WAR POET

Rob Jacques

SIBLING RIVALRY PRESS
LITTLE ROCK, ARKANSAS
DISTURB / ENRAPTURE

Sibling Rivalry Press, LLC
PO Box 26147
Little Rock, AR 72221

info@siblingrivalrypress.com

www.siblingrivalrypress.com

ISBN: 978-1-943977-29-1

Library of Congress Control No: 2016958699

This title is housed permanently in the Rare Books and Special Collections Vault of the Library of Congress.

First Sibling Rivalry Press Edition, March 2017

WAR POET

POEMS

for Ralph,
without whom not much in my life would be worthwhile

and

for my shipmates
with whom I shared duty, honor, responsibility, dedication
and love

ADMONISHING MILITARY RECRUITS

Go. Your own neighbors send you out
because some thoughts are worth dying for,
although patriotism, power, and wealth
are not among them. Go vie for us all
who believe in joy and love and Earth
tasted freely without any dogma's pall,
who believe "family" a broad, open word
inclusive of every living thing at birth.

For a time, we may be governed by idiots.
Your loyalty is never to them, your honor
never involved with their intrigues and plots.
Your worth rests alone on lovers and friends,
your sacrifice, should you make it, being one
on which not a nation, but humanity depends.

SEAMAN RECRUIT

Far away places with strange-sounding names
far away places over the sea ....
— Joan Whitney & Alex Kramer

Kansas isn't in him.
Prairies' unmoving undulations
leave him high and dry.

Prairie dogs aren't dolphins,
and chicken hawks haven't
an albatross' arousing cry.

Stationary houses aren't homes
to a soul whose urge for wander
searches for shelter that roams

from one adventure to another,
place after place, day after day,
ever at a young-hearted pace.

He sees himself in uniform,
his tight pants worn in a way
that shows off his cute ass,

attracting girls and a few boys
to a sailor with pulchritude,
romantic potential, and class.

At sea, boredom can't intrude
on a youth's desires, and waves
and wars are alike the fare

of a young seaman who craves
action for satisfaction, aware
life ashore becomes a weary slog.

The recruiter takes him in,
signs him while his brain's agog
with bright Navy blue and gold,

recruit and recruiter knowing
this much is true: when at sea,
hopes and dreams never grow old.

ANNAPOLIS

We are all beautiful in our uniforms
that cover lovely bodies only one remove
from celestial, each of us with a body
able to soothe another body, brace another soul
to face the trial of duty, honor, and the sea.

We are all beautifully uniform, cocky, plucky,
buff. Tight-lipped, tight-laced on the outside,
inside we can't get enough and are lucky
to survive the Academy's strict regimen
when all we want is to party and come alive.

We are young and trusted, hale and hearty,
eager and aware of things no longer believed
like God and country, dogma and dicta,
laud and lusty blessings given or received,
we smart, smooth future denizens of the sea.

The United States Navy wants us to be pure.
United States women (and not a few men)
want us, too, and we say "Sir!" and "Ma'am!"
when "Sir!" and "Ma'am!" should be said
this side of slaughter and creation of the dead.

Sea-warriors all, we are in training to lead
warships on perturbed waters, to dominate
outraged oceans, to perform heroic deeds
to keep civilian citizens living undisturbed
and corporations sating their reptilian needs.

Take pictures of us even if you can't admit
publicly you find us a bit erotic, a little
tempting in our incredible physical fitness,
in our soon-to-be-history innocence, in our
willingness to fight, kill, and bear witness.

A strange and narcotic thing about love:
we bond, we bind, we treat flesh savagely
in battle or in bed. We are stellar lovers
of war and subjugation, awesome actors
in the devilish play of orgasm and dread.

FIREFLIES OVER WORDEN FIELD, UNITED STATES NAVAL ACADEMY

Essentially, all poetry comes to this:
The early lines are permapressed with meaning,
acrylic at times, at times natural fiber and bold –
early lines can tear upon a mind's perusal,
tear after all into bright ribbons actually unfit for anything,
unfit strips of colors unlike the broad prose bolts so muted
that again and again say it all so well so many times over
and wear so well under abrasive eyes.
And the later lines of any poem
(the reader having gotten through the first of it all unscathed)
are simply bright bits of fabric on patterned rolls,
an unimportant image here and there badly frayed,
devoid in the end of meaning – nothing left
but garish color and rhythmic sounds by the time it's over,
sounds that'll go on onanating all night long,
or on and on as long as they're allowed to go,
for poetry is the worst form of art,
keeping its readers relentlessly searching out sense
in the deep green darkness which is, after all,
all humans know of night, and little bits and bars
of senseless brilliance that flash in the midnight's lines are,
after all, not light. No, they're just a lower life's luminescence
which fools mistake for stars.

TEACHING POETRY TO MIDSHIPMEN

Their practical minds clotted by physics and math,
their lithe bodies yearn, and while their thoughts
stay on engineering, their flesh embraces chemistry,
a hormonal bath no one duty-bound understands.

Their uniforms falsely make them appear uniform.
Though brains give orders, hearts conjure demands
unmet by Farwell's Rules of the Nautical Road, a tome
not addressing rules for bodies on a different path.

When I introduce Whitman or Cavafy and try to goad
an emotional response out of them, I get a wry laugh.
They equate warriors with winners, poets with fools,
and they can't imagine bliss that doesn't involve strife.

Their bodies can. Their bodies have the needed tools
of life to captivate, subjugate another girl or boy, and I,
an instructor who's aware of the danger found awake
in their young and lovely eyes, play it carefully, coy,

knowing they have ahead of them drills and watches,
challenges and trials, exams and careers to prepare,
but their bodies' wiles damn their naïve dedication
to seeing a glimpse of love as a safely Platonic affair.

I'll ensure they master the art of poetic explication,
readying them for a midwatch ache when lust puts
in their flesh raw desires, a mind's take on duty being
no match for a body's waking to intemperate fires.

Read subversive verses and succumb. Find a way
to compromise patriotism with sex, hostile prey with
prey not so hostile . . . willing with a bit of coaxing,
in fact, to lay down arms and lie down for an act

censorious cultures and judgmental religions ban
but which glorious bodies and elemental nature find
invigorating, wholesome with a woman or a man,
for poems require joy of a physical, radical kind.

Study them hard, those gallant poets, to finally learn
to mouth erotic language's sly labials and coronals,
say "Wow!" in fluids other than hydraulic, and
discern heaven from a sigh. Poetry shows you how.

**IN MEMORIAM for James J. Williams, Midshipman,
Who, Unable to Choose Between the Person He Loved
and the United States Naval Academy, Chose Neither
(June 19, 1950 – December 30, 1969)**

Boys of nineteen do not mourn forever . . . .
— Amy Lowell

Nineteen seventy came suddenly here.
Years, you'll admit, have a habit of coming like that
to those of us still wrapped in time and its passing.
It takes a hell of a hurt for a man to give up hope,
while Mom, Dad, and others unaware ponder and plod,
to say, "I can't cope with this. I'm not worth a damn."
It takes a sad kind of guts to drop dreams gone rotten
and in snowdrifts where summer once romped
to say to a world that ticks and tocks and talks nonsense,
"I choose to go still. I select the eternity of death."
A lot of other years wait clearing their throats in the wings
for their moment of tinsel and glitter, additional years
incessant, impatient to come, then just as impatient to go,
for the decade of the seventies is crowded by the eighties
whom the nineties nudge and won't leave alone.
Februaries forever stomp all over Januaries in their haste
to keep ahead of pushy Marches, sprinting Aprils,
and summers run after springs, jumping cues, missing marks,
forgetting lines, bulling their way through scenes,
being finally outmaneuvered by early, speedy falls.
Even those people outlasting their heartache
hurry their time along day by day into nothing.
Did you envy those grown old? Complacent, unfeeling,
gliding untouched, unharmed by passion, through years
that chronologically come to crowd out remembrance
of even classmates' names who non-alphabetically go?

Did you cry until you thought you couldn't cry more?
And then did you find that you could? Did you learn
that time doesn't pass at all, there being only one second
lasting enormously, one ache, one spasm in infinity,
one thought that ignites, stokes, strokes, feeds the burn?
Did you come to see that calendars are fairy tales,
each promised month a myth within its own religion,
each numbered day still a blank place after passage,
each square arbitrary space where time's dimension fails
at progress, change, release, evolution, hope, or grace?

What you did to yourself left poems unwritten
on your bedroom floor, in your bed. What you did
also killed your kiss, the feel of your wet mouth
and tongue given in dominance or submission
to one you love, the taste of you awakening lyrics.
Now there's much that will not happen. Closed
are possibilities that romance the mind, answers
to difficult, awkward questions your anguish posed.
Gone is the communion of your flesh with reality,
your supple body's opportunities for experience,
your curious mind's chance to grasp life in totality,
your music stopped, tune dropped, your song a gasp.

The blank canvas of your life stays blank canvas,
youth no longer evanescing about its edges as you
mature into confident understanding of yourself,
nor will awe of any kind ever again have a chance
to play in your mind for an erotic night, nor will
anything of this world ever be magical, you, lost
to quantum particles that create life's naked dance.
Rain now means nothing to you, nor will the sun
rise, set, warm or brighten your oblivion where,
for you, the Big Bang's physics has been undone.

Love would never have wanted you to die this way,
love wanting your body to revel in arousal and joy,
love wanting your mind to revel in earthy play,
love the potion that stops time cold, love the glue
that pastes the past to the present and future, love
that had hoped for a warm, fleshy, cozy home in you.

Jim, last night it snowed here, the Yard fairy-tale white
with chilled Midshipmen out in midnight moonlight
frosted alive under this newest year's large winter stars,
and the icy cold was psychotic, homicidally cruel,
sped by sociopathic winds into their bodies and minds,
and the antisocial hour grew late, hurrying time fled
as Midshipmen took in beauty that required pain to see it
believing the schemes of creation to be worth a damn,
not wanting to go back to Bancroft Hall without feeling
what time in its ever-rushing passage makes precious,
knowing no human stands unaffected in a parlous today
ever being overtaken by an unpredictable tomorrow.
Even in a crippling cold that's a sorrow, they are alive.
They are bonding to survive. They are choosing to stay.

SAILOR

Ashore, I wear my white cap jauntily to one side,
youth's cockiness making me wear my pants tight,
each port of call an opportunity to meet and greet,
love free and feckless. Underway I do my duty
for my country like all others: serving sexless,
focused on abstractions for egos, not libidos.

Underway, hunks hunker in a gray steel ship
under orders making way over oceanic oblivion
to chaos somewhere in need of gunfire or threat,
we warm-blooded boys preferring to have luck
chart all our tomorrows through war and regret
toward our body's goal of sharing love well met.

Silence about the decks! Darken ship! Belay!
In fog foggier than a brain on drugs, we ghost
nightly where no eye can see nor fingers feel,
groping for another warship groping for us,
cold metal vessels meaning to deal destruction
and death to human flesh, to love-prone flesh

that would far rather share a laugh and a beer
with other humans holding out their hands
to welcome diversity and perhaps, just maybe,
opportunities to touch and linger at the edges
of an intimacy that a wiser nature demands,
at the edges of a touching that promises much.

"Giving aid and comfort to the enemy." Or,
"Consorting with the enemy." If we were free,
we'd do more: sleep with the enemy, offer
the enemy ourselves, but instead we ride wars
and the gods we've created into blood and bone
splashed and strewn, cursed by ourselves alone.

Such pride. Such patriotic luminosity. Such
non-fraternization when human cultures collide.
Deployment ending, I return home, still alive,
still positive my own body wants to make love,
still sending signals to other bodies to share me,
couple with me, and, in spite of dogma, survive.

AN ENSIGN MEETS HIS NEW LIEUTENANT

When the earth is overcome, the stars are yours.
— Boethius

Black-eyed, black hair, dangerously cute, he's a slender gem
come to haunt my thoughts, my new division officer, and we
will deploy together surrounded closely by other men who'll
keep me chastened from which decorum, custom, and duty stem.

Every morning we're underway, I will hasten to salute him,
recognize his erotic dominance, willingly offer my submission,
ready to carry out his baritone orders, to smile, to proffer love
of obedience, of duty, of a sexuality willing to go the extra mile.

In navigating the dark through the dark, we chart tomorrow's
course over oceans indifferent to our flesh, and leaning above
his seated body, leaning as closely as I dare over his shoulder
I feel his warmth rising from his buff torso, clean and fresh.

At wardroom table, I sit beside him, my thigh negligently coy,
and, bolder, I press his leg to let him know I care, and it's with
joy I observe his indifference to my sly yet gentle pressure
for without seeming to notice anything, he leaves his leg there.

And when I hand him coffee, hand him papers to approve,
hand him anything at all, I notice our fingers touch, overlap,
and his bare hand doesn't move when I rub mine against it,
a fact that says so much to those attentive to an act so small.

I volunteer for every dirty detail he's assigned to lead, every
uncomfortable watch he's forced to stand, ready with tools,
ready with his jacket, ready with a connection turning work
into a thing grand while my dislike of arduous labor cools.

Perhaps naïve, innocent to a fare-thee-well, inexperienced
in arcane, erotic ploys of gays and straights, he doesn't grasp
the message in a lingering touch, a hankering feel, eyes
that lock eyes then are downward cast with a youthful blush.

Honest, perhaps he doesn't surmise the intent of my attention
that in older times was called a crush. His is the next move.
I won't risk overplaying my hand, thus forcing him to reprove
the intimacy with him that spices my night and fills my day.

Is he married? If he isn't, I'll make a play to earn my place
in his bed ashore where we can wrestle out of uniform
and he can get deeply into me. If he is, I know the score
and will stop at merely friendship and never try for more.

The warship of wrath and destruction and death is as well
a space of flesh and all its hormonal condiments and toys,
and steel and explosives can be softened by lusty humanity
when erotic love between two warrior men also deploys.

HARBOR HOME

Our warship lies moored within the safety of your womb,
held fast momentarily in your motherly bosom by hawsers,
nurtured and at ease with shore power's umbilical cords
that glide, then brake slightly, shift slowly, with each breeze
in the drift of a changing tide or a passing wave's brief lift.

And when our warship wends away from you in an offing
filled with trepidation and promise, exultation and grief,
imagination and duty, resignations, assignations and joys,
it's best you have a mother's emptiness at her child's loss,
a mother's ignorance of oceans to which her child deploys.

And when our warship wends away, signal flags flying,
great seabirds crying above currents of a flooding tide,
wind-blown clouds fleecy-white hying above our departing
toward wherever such ethereal ephemera go undying, we,
in our callowness, will bend ourselves to work and song.

Without us, harbor, you will be silenter, perhaps more prone
to consider those you love self-sufficient, dutiful and strong,
but we depend on the mercy of your concern, your tolerance
of the seeds we'll have sown darkly long before our return
to your shallow, safe waters with our deep, dangerous needs.

Avert your eyes. Think of our warship as your child yet.
Let your mind trip lightly along the myth of our innocence
to keep you from heavier musings conducive to guilt, regret.
Sleep. Dream of us being what you would have us be,
and if we seem strange, believe what we were in memory.

War, like love, is a rash act. War, like love, enthralls.
Predation is a fact of life that one must learn to do well,
for one must forget oneself as one must forgive oneself
when one takes leave of civilized protocols to navigate
transoceanically through war's loveless straits of hell.

In the end, we will return to you with sea stories and tales
of romance and remembrance, of hearty battles fought
by ourselves within ourselves, and may you give comfort
upon our ragged and distant return if we bring back to you
war's blood and booty when love, love was all we sought.

TAKING LEAVE OF HOMEPORT

Deploying after all, after charting and recharting stars
and courses and recourses through those stars,
provisioning and reprovisioning, planning and replanning,
plotting racetrack turns, Williamson turns, searches and screens
hard by shoals in glistening waters so remote no one dreams of seeing,
hard by islands even anal-retentive, reckless gods left nameless,
islands enough, one for every soul if ever a soul needed an island,
computing turns of a radar picket pulsing ALFA ALFA to listening silence
with so often only silence there to hear, I, fresh and feckless, blameless,
packed aboard with all lines singled up and set to cast away with one long wail,
three short blasts for backing down and backing down –
I love you, Harbor, above throbbing diesels, fires in my ship's steel stomach,
tense as I am above the many fleshy fires needing to be fed as we set sail.
You may not remember years from now, but I said it once and meant it
when I said I cared. Even while I rise and stride from your bed
my naked need to feel love stays with me very carnal indeed, my body bared,
though I and my ship go at last past telling, streaming battle flags,
our farewell into the billowing blue days riding out of harbor grace,
set to guide and drive duty's steel beneath teal skies,
wide beyond the continental shelf's outer lights and through a sounding sea.
No asters anymore, no buttercups, their yellow rich against deep green,
no wild roses left pink to blow before animal summer's thunderstorms:
gone to thoughts better not taken are yesterday's shredded flowers now,
and the seabird cries gaily and the sea-skimming bird hails us
as seasoned gray we'll go, I and my ship, life into life, duty into duty,
responsibly wind into wind, dream to deeper dreams progressing.
Beloved Harbor, when we're gone will you still remember?
When we're gone, we'll be less than echoes left from last night's prayers,
and the bells you hear are not tolling time, not in mourning,
not rejoicing, just indifferent, unconsoling measures of the sea-wind change,
and the high-rolling blue-green surf will roll as high without us,

and hot suns will still burn without us when we've gone our way:
all this encasing steel and I going to our westward furthest range.
After these callow, in-port, shallow-water days
we're getting underway, preparations done, captain watching, chaplain praying,
sailors singing those old salt songs of adventure for which we yearn.
Underway and mission-minded, sea-service strong,
we ask your blessing, Harbor. Keep a place to which in memory we may return.
Be lonely for us awhile once we're gone as a loved one should be.
Let some pier stand empty where our lines once twined the bollards
and held us briefly coupled fast beside a life-line quay,
and in winter blasts of bitterly cold days,
wrap a shawl of frost deep and shining along your wharfs to show you care.
And in some spring when thaw commands the land to life again,
dress in raucous greens the thousand trees that dress your shore.
Seeing this, others will know you remembered all the more,
and if any arousing, young rain comes along spawning in another spring
after my flesh and my steel ship ride abroad over holy ocean's foam and flare,
put some moss along the plaited anchor chains beside our open pier,
chains plaited in our gone springtime darkness, love-knots plaited half unaware.

LINES FROM THE STARBOARD WATCH

Into a warm and starlit silence drifting on a summer night,
out of a breathing stillness in a world on floating blue,
I'm watching and I'm waiting,
soft in breathing silence for a meeting in the sea.
The meeting comes, my friend, as some young love caught fresh
with stars the only lights and sighs the only sound.
I stand a watch oceans wide waiting for that one blue midnight
for dreams and daydreams to turn a steel world to flesh one time.
As the ship readies for accustomed sleep, diesels thrumming softly,
crew piped down to maintain silence about the decks,
I stand my watch regardless of the duty, mindless of the real.
Tonight I feel the dew gathering on the steel bridge rail
and long for moisture only flesh provides.
Before this meeting in a heart of quiet sea,
there is time to stand alone on summer nights
where my warm flesh and blood hears my ship's diesel heart
and paint the twin starlit voids of sea and sky in soft pastels.
Through my supple body and through my subtle fears,
through forced silence mine since birth on who I am and what I am,
I'm watching and I'm waiting.
Through a blueness and a darkness and a world aflame with stars:
a meeting in the sea.
Time is moving and I'm watching, though not always what I seem,
soft in breathing silence of an old and haunting dream.

SHIPBOARD PRIVACY

As long as the heart listens
It pumps blood.
— Harvey Shapiro

Privacy aboard ship is like god
in the universe: much sought after
but non-existent. Eyes everywhere
see other eyes roam. Whispers
are overheard by invisible ears,
and a delicate, tender touch is felt
by the ship's steel skin. Senses
aroused by endorphins are caught
by stealth electronics that detect sin.

If that third-class petty officer
who's friendly and looks so great
distracts you from your purpose,
take a shower to quickly masturbate
before you blow more than a load,
for your hands on someone to score
(other than yourself) will find you
going down a lonely, unlovely road
toward ignominy and life ashore.

Should you find aboard a buddy
who'll join you in furtive romance,
know missteps in your erotic dance
lead to career chaos, all for a chance
to do what nature demands of men,
even dwellers in the depths of the sea.
Gay sailors may stray (if they're alive)
because of a same-sex sexual drive.
Only the cautious or clever survive.

BLUEJACKET

I'm me. I'm wrapped in cotton in the cold,
a blue cotton coat my honor, my collar raised
to protect my neck, my pride on my sleeve,
my youth keeping me bold, my service praised,
I'm someone in whom my countrymen believe.

I'm you. I'm all you'd be. I sacrifice time
as you would had you the inclination to leave
the civilian world for a taste of sea salt, ships
ready to fight, fortunes that can turn on a dime,
and that heady trait of having loyalty to a fault.

I'm abstract. I'm a concept you see as real.
I'm thought made action, word made flesh,
a virtue only virtuous before war and steel
turns oaths into dying, ploughshares into swords,
and promises into froth beneath a ship's keel.

I'm solid. I'm pulchritude at its very best,
and you should see me in shower where naked
I appear to be savagely angelic, erotically buff
and still heroic, still stoic, still never at rest,
still standing guard, me, stuff of your dreams.

I'm awake. I lie abed in my ship's hard core.
I'm willing. I wait. I'm not what it seems:
I would wrestle and rub and glide on sweat
with you or an enemy toward different ends,
my body being that on which violence depends.

I'M IN LOVE WITH MY ENSIGN

Yo ho, Sebastian! Let's go far away,
somewhere where the captain won't be mad.
— Cosmo Jarvis

Freshly scrubbed from the Academy,
clean-cut to the point of being fragile,
this boy-wonder commands respect,
single gold bar aglitter on each collar,
his spit-and-polish gleaming brightly,
his creased and pressed uniform
making him appear boy-scout-ish
in the most lovely, hedonistic way.

My division officer, he shows balls
in the enormity of his self-confidence,
chief petty officers at the ready
to enforce his will. When he directs,
I respond, happy to be ordered to do
whatever he wants done, my libido
aroused to a fare-thee-well when
we brush in a ship's close quarters.

The world conspires against us:
he, an officer, me a P.O. Third,
the U. S. Navy frowning down
(although all flesh finds it absurd)
on fraternization between enlisted
and those who have command.
Few who haven't felt love's tug
could even begin to understand.

He's a sophisticated college grad
from a respected, moneyed family,
while I'm a local high school lad
from roots of poverty and slums,
and yet our bodies fit and agree,
our personalities fit each to each,
and our time together bodes well
in spite of what dogmas preach.

I stand watch with him whenever
I can, volunteer for mundane duty
if I know he's going to be in charge,
and I walk the decks with a swagger
in front of him, keeping in his view,
just happy to see him look at me
admiringly if a bit surreptitiously,
me, in my tight-ass working blues.

Mid-watch, dog watch, watching
stars align as a new age dawns,
stars laying a sheen on the ocean
through which the ship cuts anew
paths that flow wet and clean –
sometimes he joins me at a rail
and our small talk is a language
that speaks, "Love will prevail."

When standing daily inspection,
he, walking slowly along my line,
me, standing proud and stiff,
our eyes kiss for a split second
before he passes by, and I,
whether in my working blues
or starched best dress uniform,
feel possessed, clean and warm.

When he samples the enlisted
mess, he chooses my table
with never a word to me, not
even a glance in my direction,
but I feel his electric presence,
feel under his protection, feel
I'm his partner in this dance
keeping love on an even keel.

I'm proud, supple and succulent,
a "4.0" young sailor at home
on a warship with responsibilities
and a boyfriend of which others
may only dream. Of course
I love a country that gives me
liberty to become what I esteem:
to live loving, bold and free.

I wear his class ring with my tags
on a thin chain about my neck.
It bangs back and forth between
my pecs when I run, while he has
my high school picture signed
meekly "to my buddy," keeps it
in his wallet, where it rides
happily against his butt cheek.

On leave in town, he makes
reservations to play unseen
in civvies away from regulation's
undertow that would catch us
in a violent violation of which
we'd drown: in fringe hotels,
secluded pools, we meet
to make love beneath the rules.

Aboard ship, it's "Aye-aye, Sir,"
and "Permission to speak, Sir,"
and salutes rendered with respect
(and gay, manly love). But ashore,
unclothed in a hotel bedroom,
he commands with softer words,
and I give him much, still obedient
to his satin voice, silken touch.

Aboard ship, no one knows.
Aboard ship, "steady as she goes"
marks our day from reveille
to taps, to "Now, lights out.
Maintain silence about the decks,"
and I lie in my bunk awake
knowing the road we'll take,
however dangerous or dark,

will be a twining of our lives –
at some future point, human,
at some future point, open,
as every aching lover strives for
acceptance of his throbbing,
of being ascendant in the norm,
of making an April appear certain
under a February's sternest storm.

CALM SEAS

Flat, glassy seas loll sprawling around us,
and we, early to station and awaiting the fleet,
take time for swim call, netting over the side,
jumping over the side for a rare nautical treat,
bare, buff flesh flaunted with youth's pride
sporting beside our warship's hard steel hull.

Do we know the bottom is three miles down?
Do we know there's no recovery if we drown?
Davy Jones' locker lies open for one more,
always room for another sailor, particularly if
he's foolhardy and a risk-taker to the core,
if he's one who should have stayed ashore.

Rare are hours mid-ocean where calm is vast,
not the least breeze rippling holy water blessed
by an equatorial sun, and they are enjoyed
while they last, humans being human, sensory
obsessed and beautifully undressed, humans
being flesh again without mental armor's cast.

Is the cerebrum the enemy of the limbic brain?
The flesh of us would romp. The mind says "no."
The aroused animal within us yearns, while
the intellect restrains lustiness with "Whoa!"
The flesh will embrace. The flesh will love.
Only the mind sees hot passion as a disgrace.

Every human in the water wants to laugh,
and a few men furtively admire other men,
want to feel them, rub them in an ocean bath.
Noisily in a quiet sea, humanity is displayed.

Armaments and garments are abandoned while
wantonly we see male pulchritude arrayed.

Hurry, enemies. Come find us. Join us nude.
Before our fleet arrives to end this reverie
that smacks pleasantly of eroticism and peace,
come strip and play with us, our warships tense,
keeping station side by side. Release us all to
a realization that making love makes sense.

AT SEA ON A PERFECT MORNING

In starless night, ocean and sky are the same black
and my warship seems to sail through atmosphere,
no horizon, nothing to distinguish water from air,
sailing as Earth would if the Plane of the Ecliptic
suddenly disappeared, no top or bottom, up or down,
falling, rising minus reference, datum, base or crown.

Then first light, when it appears to be still night,
this deceptive lessening of black into charcoal gray,
and my warship will ride through an illusion of elision
of the boundary between the sky and sea, will glide on
as if its determined destiny weren't to awaken to kill,
as if it were human and could appreciate the dawn.

Lighter now, the division between ocean and heaven
clean, clear, azure air brighter than the aquamarine
water my warship's bow slices like the tip of a pen
laying down the stroke of a white exclamation point
sincerely intended to exclaim its readiness to erupt
noisily in munitions' smoke, death-propelling flame.

Here comes the sun. See over the three-inch turret
how molten lemon lights along an eastern sea,
sunlight shards stabbing a dazzle around mystery,
and sunlight bombards the east's horizon turning
tattered remnants of the night watch into gawking
appreciators of solar power and nuclear churning.

All the hues of blue, and only blue, ride up the sky
and paint all the sea, no other color anywhere,
except for the sun's searing, blinding yellow ball

whose light allows eyes to become useful again,
whose heat is noticed by every sailor's bare skin,
whose photons put night's dark matter to flight.

My warship's forward motion puts a warm breeze
over two twin 50-caliber machine gun mounts,
bringing me the scents of open ocean and gun oil,
and sailors doing duties about the weather decks
pause in their work to seize deeply this young day,
easy-on-the-eyes violet, indifferent to kill or play.

LOVE CALL FROM THAT SAILBOAT YOU HAD

Love isn't cast upon the waters as it once was,
back when you knew the difference between
a healthy physical strain and a migraine,
between accomplishment and mere finishing,
between day-dreaming and narcolepsy.

What happened? Where did you go?
Please don't hand me that line about aging,
for I, too, am old. The elements in us both
are older than Planet Earth and look ahead
to more cycles of redistribution and birth.

Change in you, abandonment by you,
has more to do with mind than matter,
a loss of adolescent wisdom gained
through muscle-learning, young aches
before a strong wind in a small boat.

Remember? Barefoot on a wooden deck?
My lee rail buried? A catch in your throat?
Whitecaps, small craft warnings, sea spray?
And the winch-handle's feel in turning,
and a cold wind's burning ego away?

Whatever you've done since then pales
in a memory of afternoons under sail
with a friend in the cockpit, close-hauled
on a starboard tack streaking seaward
with an active love in your young heart.

You can find me again, you know. I lie
always nearby, lines secured, ever waiting
for you to come once more, even if only
in your mind's eye, to sail me onward,
onward, loving again as you loved of yore.

SUNSET FROM A MINESWEEPER

Life's colors are deeper when seen from the sea-heart
two thousand blue miles from shore, and today,
strange as it seems to the novice unused to seeing,
the sun coming to sunset is a star of blood,
a clot from an unseen heavenly dropper dropping
toward water held in a worldly glass.
God knows why it seems that way, I guess,
and the clouds are gauze for the wound of God
who gives us this bloody sun, while the ship
seems foreign matter afloat, microscopically small,
unimportant pollutant, unnoticed unknown,
unpurified mineral unseen by God's unpracticed eyes.
With evening splattered halfway to twilight,
blood-drops hitting the sea pour platelets red in the water
scattering scarlet fluid spilled from the vascular skies.
Red in heaven's reflection, yellow in final daylight,
hemoglobin and gold billow under evening's surgical knives.
In bold incarnadine defiance of natural laws,
God's bleeding tonight, I swear, his corpuscles staining
the sea as He staunches His cut with the clouds.

CROSSING THE LINE

The crew knew before setting sail this day would come,
knew our route by heart before starting out, knew what
would happen and when it would start, knew the rules:
crossing the Equator separates Pollywogs from Shellbacks,
pulls initiates apart from veterans, and King Neptune
comes aboard to render allegiance from innocent fools,
King Neptune, a scraggily, ugly, in fact an oceanic lord.

Davy Jones has emptied his locker of playful tools:
fire hose flogs, maple syrup mixed with aftershave,
garbage to smear each pollywog's back, a flat sword
for slapping slow-moving bottoms, and, for knaves,
delicious snacks of black sea creatures eaten in front of
a shellback horde who laugh at embarrassing antics
in a maelstrom of misrule that unites as it depraves.

See the pollywog drink glop. See the pollywog eat slop.
See the Court of Neptune officiate, initiate, and bloviate
until pollywogs are left shamed and wailing in a heap,
pollywogs who've kissed the Royal Baby's belly smeared
with axle grease, swum in muck, and sung smutty songs.
King Neptune will forgive all wrongs and they will join
the Solemn Mysteries of the Ancient Order of the Deep.

Everyone's a shellback now. They sing *Anchors Aweigh*,
pledge allegiance to the flag, pray the Lord their souls to keep,
and clasp one another in renewed brotherhood, looking
toward that day when, with another crew, they will sail
across the Equator and be in charge of coercing, cursing,
harassing and haranguing innocence into experience
so in time of war's chaos a tight comradeship will prevail.

Poseidon, please forgive us. Our intent was not to mock,
but to leaven a long voyage with humor. Our rough joke
does not knock an ancient religion, and our silly Neptune
spoke only lines for laughter and pranced willy-nilly on
a warship's deck too lonesome and too advanced for sin.
Believe us. Relieve us. We are as anxious as Odysseus
and ask every oceanic god to understand all sailors are kin.

MIDWATCH, FANTAIL

Could a god come up out of it, a wake taking flight,
streaking behind us arrow-straight astern, abaft the taffrail,
an unbroken line of white disappearing into ocean night?
Neptune might not be pleased to see his sea used like this,
a warship passing to where harum-scarum destinies prevail,
its roving over the dark deep disturbing his wet-slick Nereids
as they comb his waves back, mermaids shaken out of bliss,
thrumming engines waking the dead, breaking his sleep.

Let him take me, his own naked aggression fouling ours.
Let him bear me on a seahorse beneath infinity's waves
where mermen may await me in the locker of Davy Jones.
Let them have me erotically rendered into Olympian myth
outside of space and time, making me immortal as a solace
for my possession of loves duty has rendered into stones.

A BILLY BUDD MAKES US ALL JOHN CLAGGARTS

Passion, and passion in its profoundest, is not a thing
demanding a palatial stage whereon to play its part.
— Herman Melville

Best-laid keels, like best-laid plans, can go sorrily wrong,
for ships built upon them are subject to vagaries of human hearts,
and however water-tight the transoms, bulkheads however strong,
all can be pierced embarrassingly by the unexpectedly erotic,
by longing, by yearning, by a single wistful, lustful, hurtful cry,
and war and duty can be brought down in a lover's narcotic sigh.

It takes a steel forbearance to overcome the appeal of flesh,
an almost neurotic dedication to a sublimation of desire
when sailors are young, nights are long, and needs are fresh,
when tides are strong and winds flair with testosterone afire.
It's then that a quickening pulse, eye contact held too long,
a soft brush against pulchritude give the lie to oaths men swore.

See him there, petty officer third class, savage in his youth,
feral in his raw, fleshy beauty no one with a pulse can ignore,
and you know this cruise will be suddenly cursed by a witchery
of carnal thirst that drives reason away from thought, and before
this deployment ends, you'll despise morality you were taught
and the sanctity of chastity upon which shipboard life depends.

See him bend, see him smile, see his thighs flex, his mouth form
words and words and words that arouse lust unintentionally
and your surreptitious, salacious guile, and it will take a will
impossibly beyond human strength to keep from loving him,
to keep your libido still, to keep your mind focused on duty
and your panther body away from leaping to a deadly thrill.

Why does it have to be this way? Why does this young man
have to be assigned to this one ship? But we all know the drill:
frequent masturbation, burying yourself in ship routines, and
staying your distance from this dangerous Adonis by any means,
praying he isn't sexually naïve, too. Let him know his safety
lies in keeping his eroticism under wraps and away from you.

ON DUTY AT LAST LIGHT

I have entreated you to grant me Time
To memorize the pure appointed task;
Today it is Eternity I ask . . . .
                        – Elinor Wylie

Still here. I'm still here. Cold, snow,
once invigorating, now only invigorate
the rimed trees, the frozen pond, while I,
long-practiced at this, some time ago
learned to take my ease, compensate,
hold responsibilities, hold tranquilities,
guard my life, guard the gate, guard gods,
bow down with honor, be wise, ingratiate.

Still here. I'm still here. Others go below,
leaving me the field, the deck, the conn,
the business of being, the flattery of trust.
I go on through tiring toward future sleep.
I, grown old, will not rest, will not rust.
I endure *de rigueur* in the loves I keep.

STORMY SEAS

Seen from afar, we are a small thing adrift,
a speck in an unfortunate location, the ocean
roiling white under inundations of hard rain,
an ocean flowing its might like a damning god
in no mood for reconciliation with humans,
an ocean mad with a mad sky, insane wind,
our ship steady on her course, duty-bound,
ready to brave a universe's elemental force.

That's because encased inside all this steel,
flesh exists. It breathes. It feels. It loves
itself as no other and resists logical physics
with physics of its own, logic of its own,
a warship of Cains in search of Abels, here,
alive, Eden-less in Purgatory, ourselves alone.

DAVY JONES

"Lost at sea" is a misnomer. They are not lost,
nor are they unknown to me. I watched them all,
war-tossed, storm-shriven, glide gently down
as flesh's wreckage to the sea floor, to abide
eons. I honor them. I saw them rove over oceans'
superficial surfaces and brave munitions' trauma,
a hidden reef, a typhoon's teeth, then find a grave
with me cataclysmically in my senseless deep.

Their resting place is not a shallow dot of land,
but a sea's many watery infinities, their sleep
cradled and rocked endlessly by oblivion's tide
spreading about the world their blood and bones,
their fates properly history where legends reside,
their hopes and loves now property of Davy Jones.

UNDERTOW

Drowning men know
a language all their own and those
who stand on dry land will not
hear it . . . .

— Al Maginnes

My white skin looks good against your brown,
both colors covering young muscles all red,
identical brains incautious, curious, suspicious,
both unwilling to accept a status quo, both
bound in a world hate-filled, religion-fed.

Our taut lips, yours thick and mine thin,
are ready to speak amiss, to accuse, curse,
speak outrages, spit. We could never kiss,
although I'd enjoy that more than arguing
who first did what to whom, or Holy Writ.

Our bodies want to wrestle, yours in anger
to pin me, inflict pain, slash my uniform
to a bloody robe, but mine would embrace,
hug tight your flesh, try to merge with you
after separating your body from its thobe.

You willfully will not understand me,
your stern culture forbidding even a smile
at my ready submission to your dominance,
a submission only allowed your women,
gay love an abomination, Western style.

Though you are a dark, dangerous taboo,
and my life would be forfeit should I forget,

52

I know what should and shouldn't be done.
I was made in the womb to respond to you,
though my touch would make blood run.

I refuse to hate you, hurt you, cause harm
to your religion or your world. I walk away
as you stare after, my rifle mine, my fatigues
secure, your dagger yours, your izaar tied.
Does anyone gain anything, love denied?

WARSHIP ON WINTRY SEAS

Earth's the right place for love:
I don't know where it's likely to go better.
— Robert Frost

Cryogenic winter and omnivorous seas wield
bondage, dominance and sadomasochism,
combining their cavernous austerities to make a place
on this planet like cold hollows of interstellar space.

Sleety, steel-gray atmospheres lie above and below
the sea-state-six surface where nothing living vies
with the blow of gale-force winds mixed with snow,
spume ropes whipping across storm-canceled skies.

This is ice and an ocean Amundsen knew, Nansen,
Mawson, and Robert Falcon Scott. Peary and Byrd
took a measure of freezing swells and cold winds, too,
pursuing fame through arctic weather's desolate hells,

the rimy landscape of winter seas, god-awful white,
winter seas passionless, impassive, sleet hissing
amorally with an even slight breeze stinging anything
unfortunate enough to be alive in a winter sea's bite.

Gray, too, and just as cold, a steel hull cuts through
swells and spume, a keen shape rigged against
sharp weather, tossing seawater skyward either side
of a clawing, cleaving warship's abrupt geometries.

Her canted decks shed the freezing swells washing
stem to stern. Her weapons are ice-encrusted.
Her stanchions and cleats, anchor chains and truck
are coated with glare-ice sheeting and ribbon stains

from blown-back diesel exhaust slammed down
on her decks from her engine's sloped funnels,
diesel fumes unfurled, whipped and whisked
backward into the oblivion of this frigid world.

But winter isn't an accursed thing, nor does the sea
harbor enmity, nor does this warship hunt on its own;
rather, as in all things, perception and purpose fall
to warm, soft flesh – vulnerably human and alone.

In the eyes of the ship, on the impervious bridge,
see where blood and bone wrestle with etherealities
of their own spinning, creating internal, mental weather
made from good and evil, obedience and sinning.

In the ship's inner sanctum, where warm flesh resides
with warm flesh close by, see where love has potential
to thrive in proximity to propensities that kill. In this,
as in all things, it's human will that ultimately decides.

VICE ADMIRAL HAROLD G. BOWEN, JR., REFLECTS

MacArthur was right. We never die. We fade,
serenely silent, watching, but still fire-horses
made ready by any alarm, on still-steady legs
supremely confident we kept history's course
from veering into mediocrity . . . or worse.

So many years, so many years: tennis, cocktails,
my evenings reminiscing what was then and how
it could've been better than what we have now,
my life is a rest and recall of those bright days
pledged to honor and country, Navy and praise

of Lawrence's words bannered in Memorial Hall.
As a sworn midshipman passing day and night
by that immortal call, what possible thoughts
could I have had for popular press, eager media,
or safe civilians who never face battle death?

Bucher's tears, his coddling ways, a father
to his men, a father he never had, played well,
entertained people in their living rooms
still in the wrenching grip of unpopular war,
seeing in weakness a salvation, not doom.

Here at Fort Myer, rectitude is still precious,
and at the Officers Club we carry ourselves
upright with a spare dignity earned through
sacrifice gallantly offered. Heroes-in-waiting,
every one of us would've fired and died.

I heard the grave pundits, read the newspapers,
how he saved eighty-two lives by surrender.
My God! How do they know? What would
one shot have done? One act of resistance?
But one must not speculate. One must bow.

Here in the Old Guard Lounge, I await doubles.
Time has passed on, tennis courts replacing
courts of inquiry, scotch whiskey replacing
shipboard water, former comrades-in-arms
replacing duplicitous politicians and failure.

Today, my partner and I try for a trophy,
his service, my backhand and smash
together making light work with volleys
where life comes down to a game,
much reduced from actual battle's clash

where honor can fall before media follies
and fame and glory rest on shoulders
that shrug off self-discipline and duty.
Where is he now? Whom does he regale
with his take on pathos and romance?

How many more lives are now at risk
in a world where pirate states await
softness, self-pity, and libertine ways?
Sparta knew a thing or two about warring,
wearing shields or being borne upon them.

Enough. The world is now less safe,
our modern civilian leadership less sage.
I spend mornings, afternoons at games,
glad to be no longer tempted to storm
Wonsan Harbor and clean honor's page.

WAR POET

Not an oxymoron, contradiction in terms,
I am what I am, solemn, stressed, proud.
Glory and shame are my oil and water,
battle my canvas: open ocean or city street
or dark cellar where hell awaits replete
with all manner of devilment allowed.

My verbs jangle brutal Anglo-Saxon
with beautiful Latin. My rash nouns
are serviceable good and bad, often clashing,
often bloodied, wounded, fouled with filth,
often given to bodies flayed, de-limbed, disemboweled,
often death watches sitting awhile on a medic's shoulder
before suddenly spreading wings and descending.

I pen medals appropriately enough
in highfalutin language suitable for framing,
for cutting into brass or iron or stone
or even marble. The praise I give is universal
for the fallen everywhere. My inspiration
comes from heroes and their long pull
from beginning of combat to the end,
from beginning of death to the end.
My images do not do justice to the actual
bayonet plunge, its twist, its awful twist,
its slicing viscera into red-pulp tripe.

Don't turn away! Give violent work respect.
You pacifists make me sick, your puling
as if nothing were fit to die for,
as if submission were victory of sorts,

tolerance not loss, cowardice pretending to be nice.
You would have us all die in bed for nothing,
but I tell you those who hold still
never know the rush, the honorable horror,
the cause enshrined in a family's plot,
whose name cut into fearsome stone
with birthday and death-day
translates "You have no idea."

ODE TO WAR

A bare-chested boy in pajama bottoms, barefoot,
wearing a paper hat jauntily askew, a proud smile,
stands in his bed straddling his equally clad friend,
boys in the midst of a sleepover arranged by parents,
wooden swords in their hands, their worlds in clover.

Life is good, so far. So far, this bedroom skirmish,
mattress-padded and dreamy with a myth of victory
and small and painless and unimportant defeat,
this tussle on clean, white sheets bounded by friendship
and its rules and intimacies and selfless clamorings,

has not drawn blood. Nor will it, the boy on top
already sliding down beside the boy lying supine,
their swords slipping dully to the carpeted floor,
one boy giggling as he claims his momentary win,
the other already in sly thought of a counterplot.

An innocent beginning, War, and you must do better.
They must be taught heroics. The possibilities of
technologies used for patriotic purposes. Superiority
of everything their country holds dear. War, you must
be sure their love does not ever overpower their fear.

ANTI-SUBMARINE WARFARE

be careful about getting hung up in the brain's things
that send you screaming like madmen through the town
— Miller Williams

Sunlight and shadow play along ocean surfaces, sunlight shallow,
not penetrating to depths I need to know as I pore over
a ghostly ocean's foam, pale and slight, pale and leeward blown,
spindrift sparkled by sunlight, silver-dollar sparks flung among
the tossed dross of a white-feathered sea fluttering about me,
silver dollars blown across the bone in my ship's steel teeth,
strewn as gloss over my ship's straight and wind-whipped wake.
Through winds of the world grown furious, the world mad,
the world knowing only black and white, I ply for its sake
across ocean with little in the offing I could offer as my own.

All knowledge relevant is coded in cloth taken from canvas bags,
strung along wind-ripped halyards, in mute gale-wracked flags
that snap and flap their colors, their naval language, their cries,
silent cries, to no one in particular and everyone in general
out here hunting as I hunt, watching as I watch, for the prize
of finding fathoms down a master-maker of blunt-force trauma
hiding in the depths of some other wrathful country's despair.
I read meaning sent abroad from young signalmen working
a quiet communication between ships, their tight uniforms
wind-tightened more, communicating with a subtle, erotic flair.

Hot and cold, hot and cold go the sonar scopes, sweep-sweeping
around and around as I grow old waiting in a hollow steel box
atop what the Navy hopes is a foolproof hunting machine.
Whip-whip go the radars, about and about, I, looking at what
each pass brings, feel wet emptiness below and fall to thinking
about the milk of human kindness and such subjective things.

I will be here forever. I am here searching even in my dreams.
I am mindless of the Big Picture, the animosities, the practice
of seeing good and evil as separated into opposing teams, and I
tire, ache and tire. I would say whatever the sin, love redeems.

I think of you at a bad time, the compass shouting and shouting
and still lying, for I'm not here, not heading there, not free
to choose. Sometimes it seems whatever choices I'm permitted
to make, I still lose. Lost, I'm harmless to enemies of the state.
Lost, I'm dangerous to the rigorous right. Who in their sane mind
allowed me authority to command? I did not consecrate my life
fully enough to dicta and dogma to kill on demand. I have not
passion to will the deaths of industrious haters lurking below.
I tinker on a bridge guiding profound weaponry through the blue
and respond rotely, dutifully, though to my humanity I be untrue.

When I close my eyes to the ship, the laws, and the crew, I find
for moments I can be with you in your own cultural strictures
as you hunt me, too. Aren't we alone together? Haven't we
means, motive and opportunity to commit the crime? Wouldn't
you torpedo me as easily as I might stop to depth charge you?
Are you as aware as I that the nights are short, so short, and
so quickly pumped full of love? They're suddenly, irretrievably
gone, those warm, wet human nights so dear, leaving us frothed
into forgetting the joys of orgasm are greater than the pleasures
of war. Must we spurn heaven, turn to a hell lasting forever here?

THOUGHTS FROM THE BRIDGE
OF A HUNTER-KILLER DESTROYER

Oh who can tell the range of joy
Or set the bounds of beauty?
— Sara Teasdale

Our erotic savagery rides long-striving under and above black sea waves.
Our twin midnights glide about us soundlessly, hiding away from starlight
as we feel delicately, touch gently, move dangerously through dark water.
He's baptized to a sanctioned mission, blessed for a sanctified purpose
as am I, both of us sworn to stark duty in our respective national churches,
novitiates to war's cardinal-red religion, our hard bodies primed, both of us
made as fresh tools yearning to find each other using our tricks of the trade
to prove technology's law of natural selection, survival of the fittest flesh.
My body, like his, is firm, warm inside a steel cage. My body, like his,
wants what it wants and accuses common sense of lying. My body, like his,
is a prisoner of the mind, unfree to romp in orgiastic, orgasmic joys, but
our bodies pray and prey, hunt and are hunted, give and get, are at once
both tools and toys, our minds whispering "Tomorrow," our hearts shouting
"Today!" And here we are shunted away from loving onto a watery course
of hide-and-seek where death is, though death does not speak. Death
knows no resurrection of the human heart, knows with enough holy water
even bishops drown, knows no afterlife afterward, knows no erotic
blossom bosomed in torsos intertwined in bed, knows only mortification
of everything living as it removes passion from the perpetuity of the dead.

Who are we? Who are we, really? We are forced to feel each other
electronically, never sharing a culture or a touch, let alone an embrace
that might shatter dogma and dicta, human civilization, time and space.
You, far below my gliding keel, my muscled missiles, my muscled arms,
wait for your moment to strike and disappear from this killing place,
hoping your sudden torpedoes won't set off my ship's warning alarms.
But I offer you solace, you who curse me vengefully without reason:

Know ever after we are married to each other in this wicked moment,
our vigil above and below blessing a marriage that began as stardust
eons ago, atoms made in stars improbably coming together here and now
to do to each other that which our belief systems say must be done.
Yet I would hold you gently, firmly, and make love. And kiss you,
yes, kiss you, though you might not mentally cope. Love demands it,
love requires I be true, for in that last carnality lies all there is of hope.
For heaven's sake (and our own), come kiss me savagely, you whose atoms
have journeyed here from all time past and who has wanted this meeting
in just the same way as a bridegroom traces the location of his dear,
finding love's body naked and aroused, grabbed bare-ass and sweating,
stabbed wet with a whetted weapon and purpose in a room full of fear.

COMBAT INFORMATION CENTER

Who shall set a law to lovers?
Love is a greater law unto itself.
                              — Boethius

In the blinding dark, secreted away from harm
lies a space, a brain where all signals from all senses
come for sorting, then reacting at the first alarm.
Hidden apart from the main controls of a ship's bridge,
this is a sunless place without windows: electronics,
charts and dials being eyes, ears, nose, tongue and hand
sending out responses against supposed threats and trials
perceived, received, plotted, analyzed and scanned.

Here in the binding dark we do what killers, lovers do:
murder and create, grab and hold down, minding only
our tempestuous flesh, our fear of an enemy's knife,
our skittish fetishes about domination ruling our clay,
our warrior life keeping us in uniform when we'd rather
be naked, make love, stop being our own harm's way.

GUANTANAMO

I'm trying to get the terrorist out of the bugaboo category
and into the category of a fellow human being.
— John Updike

Not pits in the earth in Boko Haram's northeast Nigeria,
nor holes in the sand in ISIL's Syrian lands, nor yet
cold caves in Taliban-controlled Afghanistan, nor even
hot cellars in Yemen where Al Qaeda's hate is whet,

not anywhere but the Americas does this place exist
without irony or shame, a space reserved for those
who resist one culture or another, violent, dangerous,
who believe the innocent have their share of blame.

What to do, what to do? For if the truth be known,
they'd kill truth, too. They are lightning in a bottle.
They are made dark. They are what has been sown.
Whatever is Western is tinder. They are the spark.

Do roosters willingly harbor hungry, angry foxes?
Do rats willingly succor ravenous, venomous snakes?
Holding the proverbial tiger by the tail, how does one
let go without that becoming the biggest of mistakes?

Magic is needed where blood is up and demanding,
nor is it helpful to speculate and calculate the odds,
for miracles are not beyond a heart's understanding,
nor are black curses infinite from anyone but gods.

WAR AND PEACE, THE SONNET

The world's Rostovs get by, Nikolais and Natashas
always naively believing the world's Napoleons
will keep still, Kuragins only scheme harmlessly,
and Dolokhovs may not, after all, kill. Pretty Borises,
intelligent as well, prevail in love and economics
while old guard Bolkonskis hold cultures together
as the world's liberal Pierres foment for reform and
young tsars battle desperately to maintain the norm.

But old generals like Kutuzov know the people,
ah, the people, blow hot and cold across history,
laugh and let blood, history later creating events,
heroes and villains. Kutuzov drinks his vodka,
accepts young women and fate, knowing folly is
human, is pride, is a contagion nothing prevents.

KITTY HAWK

. . . great stretches of water and sand dunes and beach
and a tremendous sky overhead, with cumulus clouds
rising like castles, thrilling to behold against the blue.
— David McCullough

North Atlantic seasonal savagery ravages these banks,
sandblasting chaos, dunes adrift amid ranks of American
beachgrass, dunes shadow-casting onto stretches of land as
sunlight, moonlight, night and day twirl, pass, as wind lifts
grandly, flings fine sand into rippled drifts, swings inward
in gales for miles raising sand hills far away in brine spray,
and a cold, blue sky oversees it all, cirrus, cumulus clouds
conjured up, risen in tumult, blown fits of white and gray.

Something happened here. Time has forgotten what it was:
a man, a mechanic of matter, and a slim splinter of a thing
flickered thinly, crane-fly-like and harmlessly, in space
previously unoccupied by the human race, and then gone.
Breakers break where once ephemerally creativity was done
by a species, and North Atlantic ocean thunder rumbles on.

SENTIMENTAL SENTINEL

It is no small labor to rescue all mankind,
every mother's son.

— Homer

This horrible job in this horrible place
is made no easier by time with myself
during which I idle, I pray. Given space,
I play God. In the Eden of my mind's dark,
I wonder who my enemies are. I have
orders. I am armed with sharpened steel.
My bayonet's snicker-snack would mar
would-be attackers with penetrating zeal.

But I'd rather not waste existentialism
bred of isolation in this languorous night,
its operatic potential, its ability to heal.
Are you an enemy? Behave irrationally
and I'll join you in a disarming madness.
Set down your weaponry, forget your kills.
Let me touch you slowly, softly, charming
you, teaching you love's diplomatic skills.

Let our masters sleep soundly and safe
while I, on watch to defend sacred honor,
get naked to show you how harmless I am,
place your hands on me, my hands on you,
kiss you so you'll know love is alarmless,
bless you so you'll know our God is great,
send you smiling back to your side with
no demands after hatred's failed attack.

And in the morning, having made love
not war, in the morning when others rise
to greet us and hear how the night went,
I will say your people are heaven-sent,
you tell your people my people are wise,
we two beginning an education of armies
about how making love is healthy, we,
built to come together over dogma's lies.

LOVE SONG FOR A RUSSIAN ATTACK SUBMARINE

Call us what you will, we are made such by love.
                                    — John Donne

Up here on the unreliable surface of things,
in spindrift-laden winds of a brewing storm,
whitecaps wave white warnings, spume scudding
airborne over me, overarching my ocean view,
and tossed about lonely and alone I hunt for you
who waits below, silent, deadly in tint and tone,
who waits I know for common sense to take over
to make a world that we may be harmless in together,
lusty without iron and steel, just blood and bone.

I wait expectant. I hold my breath in howling air,
on gale-blown seas, within a bridge's cavernous dark
listening for a ping, looking for your blip to indicate
fathoms down from me you are there. You, too, hark
to hear my thrum above you, and I will have you
soon or late, obviously or secretly, in your water lair,
you prostrate beneath my keel, inviting with each tick,
each knock, each echoing sigh imagined or real,
my full attention to your every obfuscating trick.

Anticipating your move, I wet my lips, needles dance.
I close my eyes to better feel my diesel engine's throbs.
Shy antics like yours make my time hard. Sonar knobs
tuned to hear you, my sensors alert as if in a romance,
subtle skin along my sides turned to feel your heat,
60-beats-per-cycle my sonobuoys pulsing, matching
the pulsing of my heart, I want you to sense me here
waiting and certain of contact between us, your
shielding water curtain no barrier to seeing a peer.

My thoughts are where my hands would be. Could be.
Should be, if there were any sense to any of this.
Both of us steeled to our purpose, we do this dance,
you and I, keeping the faith by stealing quietly
above and below, around and about, target to target,
and we do a do-si-do. I'd end this stand-off stance
if I could, my hands my only weapons holding you
down, my lips, my teeth, my tongue instructing you
in how a fleshy mouth makes better love than war.

I will take love where I find love, having spent much,
endured much, demanded much, finding prudishness
obnoxious, chastity unnatural, abstinence toxic. I watch
your slender shape in my mind's eye, you beneath me
while I ride, mouth agape, stormily over your steel,
you helpless to prevent it, you complicit in this affair,
both of us enjoying what we both feel, both of us
in command to do and dare, ready in a heartbeat to act,
the situation critical, flesh never happy with a even keel.

Waves that toss me, cause my ship to rise, waves
spraying salt water splashings as high as my bridge,
waves of energy, waves of force under a sodden sky,
do they reach you down there? Are we both slaves
to white-water weather's buffetings, you rolling through
energy's undulations as if you, too, were caught as I?
You, too, captive in an ocean of life's roil and boil?
You, too, willing (if you could do so discreetly, neatly)
to give yourself to victimless lusts without regret's soil?

Haven't you desires you crave to sate? Sleek, bold, you
must have urges fanning flesh's fires barely controlled.
What would be my fate if others knew how much I care?
I feign ignorance of your presence, order the helmsman
to turn this way or that, my ship's engine order telegraph

set to all ahead slow, my ship's screws turning above
your alert body lying with your long, quiet weapon abed,
and I would give the world to wrestle you down, you,
someone else's enemy reduced, seduced to making love.

RUSSIAN CAPTAIN OF THE FIRST RANK

We have been commanded to be friendly,
allowed to be officially nice, affable even,
permitted to smile, shake hands, and share
sea stories, strong coffee, a bit of chess,
the Russians cleared to visit our bridge,
crew's quarters, gun mounts, and mess.

I stand by, ready to show where we sleep:
hard, cold, closed-in-steel berthing racks
keeping men separated, isolated by two feet
and are a cinch to bail out of whenever
an enemy attacks. My gray locker is open
for inspection, personal items displayed.

And then in he comes, hatless, smiling,
in hot lead of his official touring parade,
and while his buff body is solidly built,
his face is youthful, delicate, eyes black,
his two-day growth of beard stubble
on such a boyish face taking me aback.

He smiles slyly as he sees me react
to his dominant, masculine good looks,
his eyes running over me, up and down,
as I smile, too. I shyly, softly explain
in English that is being translated for him
what worlds our ship's spaces contain.

For my supple, slender body's language,
he will need no translator, for my flesh
responds to his fresh masculinity minus
today's politics, religion, or cultural norm,
me, doe-eyed, sheepish, and submissive;
him, a muscular, wolfish, dominant form.

Listening to me with a slight, dimpled smirk
shows he knows. Fragile dogma and dicta
evaporate in an instant before our urges
of healthy eroticism millions of years old.
Done, I let him brush against me as a tease
showing our mutual liking, both being bold.

"Please take me with you, my Captain,"
I dream of saying, "and I'll be subordinate.
I'll serve you always faithful, completely."
I would learn Russian, adopt his customs,
settle somewhere in his cold austere north,
demonstrate nakedly, fully, my loving mettle.

And now I think I've been too long at sea,
And now I know I need to find my own mate
with whom to do what comes so naturally:
care for him, share with him, rub, copulate.
Testosterone is a determined master, mighty,
unsubjugated, unregulated even in ships at sea.

PORT OF CALL

I came upon it from a tussle with the sea—
and I was young—and I saw it looking at me.
— Joseph Conrad

Literally, figuratively, sugar and spice.
A world away from normal, I'd be released
to swirl naked in my young independence,
a beast alive to my fleshy senses, a lover
of that native woman, this indigenous man,
lying athwart sweat-wet sheets after play
that recompenses me for duty, valor, God
and country, sin now virtue, pornographic
now merely erotic-artistic, my parents' chaste
son erased in iniquity so graphic, palpable,
and narcissistic, civilization comes undone.

I would gaze out from the ship's steel rail
at a land so strange that I would have nothing
in common with its people outside of loving,
outside of surrender, religions to no avail;
a land of change, a people of sensuous mien,
and I would look furtively at a buxom miss,
size up a slender guy, go ashore to lose myself
in her breasts, in his junk, high on sex's
inebriation, drunk with reproductive fluids,
milk, cream, our bodies slick with each other,
physically exhausted with our eyes agleam.

I would, years from now, an old man lying
ill in some chaste, regret-filled room, recall
once upon a time in decades flown and
nations long ago lost to civilization, recall

once upon a time I loved without chains,
without artifice and artificial hindrance,
and though nothing of her or him remains,
I would at my dying want to fail and fall
into a moment's heaven remembering bliss,
a boy's blush, a girl's kiss. Port of call,
so mysterious, so imperious, grant me this.

IT'S A PHYSICAL WORLD

This candied Earth is everything your body wants,
your hot flesh seemingly made for this treasure.
You could not have designed a body any better
to play hastily, taste and see, to feel and smell,
to rub and hear, stroke, grab ahold and cuddle
all you could have wished for as you formed

in the motivating womb. For your muscles, bone,
Earth is a mating feast of biblical proportions.
For your too-ready senses, it's a tingling delight,
no young green going unenjoyed, no old brown
going by without frowning recognition of time's
slow passing away out of sight and out of breath.

Nothing can make you happier than your body.
Nonjudgmental flesh knows to have a good time,
its all-inclusive appetites ready to raid, indulge,
molest savagely, tenderly (whichever's appropriate
at the moment), ready to undress in a heartbeat,
ready to undress a willing Earth for tussling love.

Mother Nature wants you to enjoy your body even
as it's being enjoyed by amoral marauders higher up
on the economic food chain, social food chain,
political food chain. Sensuality reigns on Earth
up and down energy and matter, quark after quark
assessing all others for possibilities of union, love.

While your body giggles, jiggles like a besotted tot
at the splendid things it will do and do if left
to its own caressing, endorphin-seeking devices,

its own urges giving excess and license the nod,
what does your mind tell you? Yes, your mind.
Your mind understands this is the problem of God.

UP EARLY AFTER LOSING HIS INNOCENCE,
THE BOY WATCHES THE SUNRISE

> *. . . so many stars*
> *and so few hours to dream. . . .*
>
> — Carl Sandburg

Coming up gold east of Eden, lightening sand, tinting rock,
a chastising, chastening sun hastens liberal night westward,
and the newly experienced boy sees. It's as if blinders
have fallen from his still-aroused eyes, and there before him
day flies forward, onward, over landscape heretofore unknown,
but now forbidding, foreboding, that will forever be his own.

Was it honor-bright Lucifer whose showy scintillations slowly
lessened into shadow, dimming after his sin of pride, his white
evanescing into red desire, his heart a home now to black fire?
The boy remembers morning's mirror where he saw himself
undazzled. What last evening had been a wonderful country
was reflected as a desert in his mind's eye, a promise unraveled.

All he had known was seen anew through a lens now error-prone.
Everyone goes down this way. Everything is Ecclesiastes.
Song of Solomon followed by Leviticus, then Lamentations.
He would not go back, though, even if he could, for five senses
outweigh whatever philosophies may devise and flesh follows
clay down finally to the point where nothing more can surprise.

They say the land of Nod had little to recommend it, yet Cain
wandered there making the best of it, marrying his sister Awan,
building a city for his son Enoch among the alluring and profane.
Did he forgive himself for being what he had become? Did he
justify what he'd done to himself? As he wandered life,
did he see himself damned or a man? Driven or drawn?

Innocence can be lost but once, its disappearance delicious,
though ignorance, purity, and mystery are impossible to regain,
and having eaten from the tree of knowledge of the difference
between good and evil, one expects pleasure followed by pain.
Innocence can enjoy nothing, holy though it is. Experience
is the measure of going from fire to ash with wisdom as gain.

The boy is soiled now, a bit used, slightly spoiled, a touch
abused, no longer fresh, but his curiosity is far from sated,
mythological night having yielded to action-brightened skies,
and his flesh, while stung, is elated. He'll do it again. Hell
has fallen. Heaven awaits creation. He's a man this morning,
the sun finding him more complicated, implicated, wise.

METAPHOR

With a steady wind of twenty boisterous knots,
spume speeding airborne aft across the deck,
the slick hull slicing with a hiss, taut rigging
singing a thin hymn to a bracing day at sea,
the shiny teak tiller requiring both my hands
(and then some) to make the rudder stay true,
the sleek beauty of my long daysailer cutting,
close-hauled, scudding away from safe lands,

I now realize my boyfriend is my sailboat,
being lovely to stare at, to feel doing what
he does so well, slender and supple, he also
an impractical, expensive joy to ride, but
worth it for the thing at which both excel:
arousing me handsomely to a fare-thee-well.

PEARL HARBOR

Did something happen here? Long ago
hatred blew apart sanity in an enterprise
opening a new sad chapter in madness
that won't be done until humanity dies.

You can number the dead. Memorials
are everywhere a testament. This or that
memory still recalls. Children yet learn.
Citizens turn to holidays to deck the halls

where lie the killed with flags and flowers.
Memorial Day. Veterans Day. Perhaps
Thanksgiving? How long will it go on?
This reverence for the viciously slain?

Sanctity for sites of psychotic slaughter
where humans took leave of their senses
for war before once again becoming sane,
sanctity for spots to commemorate gore

are good only for a time of healing pain,
and then nature honors what was before:
palms sway along an Edenic fringe of bay
where tropic sun enchants new humans

to romance, to play, to lie in warm sand
naked with each other and make love,
seawater for swimming bare together
sparkling with the sun's ubiquity above.

Where have they gone, these heroic lost?
Wherever they are, go and ask them now
if honor and principle were worth the cost
of sea and sun and air, and ask them how

oblivion compares to being alive, aware,
to horizon-less curiosity and oceanic sky.
Little lagoon, Navy-wrapped, sailor-strong,
was there a yore of pre-civilization when

humans made hefty love in your waters,
sin not yet discovered, right and wrong
matters of the heart and not dogma, with
love, love never an occasion for regret?

THOUGHTS ON A SUICIDE BOMBER'S COWARDICE

Here, in the deepening blue of our corruption, let
love be at least one corruption we chose together.
                                                    — Carl Phillips

The fleshy thrill of 72 virgins not being enough
to overcome the spiritual chill of sudden death,
you balked, begged, bared your vest to us, and
somehow we didn't shoot you. Your young eyes
caught mine, your fright and tears touched
my own, your youthful tenor cry awakening
the thought, there but for the grace of God go I.

Young man, you're a strange thing sitting here,
handcuffed, chained, stripped bare. How easy
it'd be to send you back from whence you came:
they would surely kill you. There, other fanatics
would wield the whetted knife: snicker-snack!
and then your head would roll out bleeding life,
your healthy body coated hopelessly with red.

Our gods have put us here, done this to us,
yours as unforgiving of life's soft blasphemies
as mine, mine as hateful of impiety as yours,
neither willing to leave us alone to flower.
Both would have us kill and kill and kill until
the human race breeds automatons, myrmidons,
the planet quiet, the ungodly a past disgrace.

Thank you for not killing me. Thank you
for not dying. Ah, Love, I would bathe you,
salve your interrogation's welts and wounds,
take off your binding cords, have you trust

in what your body believes. Our soft bodies
don't want to die. They fight our hard minds
that would sacrifice us all for someone's lie.

LOVE'S TRIAGE

Who will live, die? Who has,
in a war with limited resources,
the best chance to survive?
The head does the mathematics,
assesses probability, knows odds,
while whatever the cold choice,
awful figures placed on paper
chill, deaden, depress, debase.

But the heart calculates otherwise,
uses soft numbers whose origins
are not Arabic, nor Roman,
nor Boolean logic's zeros or ones,
and looking into this one's eyes
dispenses medicine that love gives,
the head insisting, this one dies;
the heart resisting, this one lives.

MAN OVERBOARD!

Great God! This is an awful place . . . .
— Robert Falcon Scott

This hasn't yet befallen, happened to you,
shock and horror, mouth-drying fright,
a bowels-loosening, uninterrupted sight
of ocean three-hundred-sixty degree blue
with nothing, nothing, nothing at all,
so you don't dare laugh at the thought,
for this is an isolation unbelievably vast,
fraught with agony sufficient to stab, appall.

It's a two-o'clock-in-the-morning nightmare,
though you lie fast awake in your bunk hearing
heart-beat-like thrumming of friendly engines
assuring you it's no mistake: you're safe aboard.
Still, you know you're but a misplaced chock,
an unnoticed cleat, a misstep into a scupper, or
an inopportune turn over a stanchion or block
before you're meat thrown to fishes for supper.

A bump, innocent or otherwise, on a night-dark
weatherdeck already slick and aslant in rain,
and you (when you finally surface gasping) see
a stern light moving away at speed, the sound
of prop wash and diesels lessening, and water,
water being not one of the things you need, you
know you will eventually drown, but you don't
believe it. You won't believe it until you do.

You're healthy. You're young. You're screwed.
You scream. In fact, you shriek. You can float
if you don't panic. For hours with hope renewed.

But you can depend on what will happen in awhile,
painfully drowning in the end, a merciful minute
once it's begun, or you can just do it now, diving,
exhaling air, inhaling sea, stopping the fright by
giving up, stopping the fight, accepting eternity.

In daylight, it's fifty-fifty you'll be found alive.
In the night, your percentage is less than five, but
if you beat the odds, you'll be held and hugged
by sailors who silently share this worst of fears,
and you'll swear to be more careful next time
you're on a weatherdeck when bad weather nears.
Note to self: wear a life jacket with a pocket flare, too,
and stay on good terms with even a mutinous crew.

SEXTANT

. . . you and your crew may still reach home,
suffering all the way, if you only have the power
to curb their wild desire and curb your own.
　　　　　　　　　　　　　　　　 — Homer

While your mind may wander anywhere,
your body must be somewhere. Trust
electronics at your peril, remembering
overconfidence turned the *Titanic* to rust.

Let imagination take you far from this sea,
but always be prepared to find out where
you really are, your ephemeris your bible
to interpret your location using every star.

It's like your heart tells you you're in Eden,
its fruits yours to eat when you deploy, but
your head calculates a position much truer
with more duty, more blue and gold, less joy.

Celestial navigation is a bore. No one
wants to learn the humbling, accurate score.
We all would rather wish upon a star
and not know the truth where we really are.

For instance, this young quartermaster
in his ass-tight working blues makes a heart
beat faster as he helps you shoot the moon
to learn your datum and make guesswork moot.

You'd rather rub against a buxom bosun
than not, but the sextant in your brain plots you

standing just this side of catastrophe if you
don't refrain. It allows you to connect the dots

that place you ethically in jeopardy as well as
physically in parlous seas, and no dead reckoning
however skilled will save you like a sextant
from running aground in situations like these.

WASHING MY ENEMY'S FEET

I hold his foot gently. I know it hurts. I try
to soak sore places of abraded skin, soothe
oozing wounds with my fingers, cleanse
his broken toes, bleeding heel and arch
as each of us peers at war through a different lens.
My hands' touch, as close to love's caress
as it could be, is a soft physical submission
upon which real communication depends.

We'd laughed when we learned of his stupidity:
after planting his IED craftily, surreptitiously,
in the roadside dark, he tamped down
the ground around it with his foot. Embedded
rock sent the force of the blast away from him,
torn muscle here, bloodied skin there, but
he survived remarkably well, his screams
alerting intended victims he had a story to tell.

His black eyes follow me. His feet are dark
with clots, scars, sand and dirt, a few pebbles
blasted into his insteps and ankles. He's
angry that we, his targets, see him as a fool.
We may be fools, too, for we won't kill him.
He'll be beaten, questioned, beaten, questioned
and beaten again before his release places us
on a path to meet once more down the road.

This is somber, sober work—this disinfecting
of flesh that wants me dead. Even now as I
massage his ankle, I know that what I want
to believe is a smile is probably a sneer, and yet

I wish him no harm. I'm a lowly soldier
(a lousy soldier?) relishing an act of mercy,
performing a duty with humanitarian charm,
the ambiguity of which he's partially aware.

Were it not for cruelties of war and worship,
I'd strip him bare, make my cleaning complete,
washing, salving, salvaging his naked soul.
The Pope and his bishops wash pre-cleaned feet
for holy paparazzi—and I'm sure an ayatollah
or two would be as kind—but dirt and blood
and hatred leeching from maddened eyes
demand we wash with a lover's state of mind.

LOVE CALL OF A U.S. NAVY FRIGATE

When you were here in me, you were young,
your eager body doing everything you told it to.
Discipline? Your callow body had it. Hunger
for every experience was the order of the day,
and I satisfied that gnawing hunger in spades.

We were unabashedly raw, raucous, tough
and cute, both of us certain, mettle meets metal,
me, hard-hot weapon, you, soft-lithe recruit,
and we pretended they'd be no bygone days,
that our youth-soaked adventure would go on.

Remember my diesel thrum, from my truck
the transoceanic view of horizon-to-horizon
desire. Remember, too, how your heart burst
on my weatherdeck, night exploded with stars,
endless wind-ripped opportunities alive, afire.

Achilles in his chariot, Odysseus at his helm,
Hercules muscling through his labors, metaphors
of you at this one time in your spanking-new life
when you envied no god, begrudged no one joy,
fell asleep to aspirations ringing in your ears.

Together we rode high seas until ripe China,
Malaysia, Indonesia came nigh, and you
bathed yourself in the oils of their offerings,
sweetnesses stripping off your virgin's clothing
as they have bared young sojourners in all times.

Gunfire! Cover your ears! Get up high on me!
Cheer! Man overboard drill! Williamson turn!

Steady on the reciprocal, and there he be! Pull!
With tenderness and much touching charity,
bring him back aboard! Hot coffee! Cup full!

The coffee was nectar, the food was ambrosia,
the crew fast friends, the command an authority
whose every challenge was doable, the goal
clean and good as no goal ever would be again
because your innocence was supple and fresh.

You kept me well-fought and maintained, oiled,
scrubbed, polished, and though you were flesh
I liked you smeared with grease, usefully trained,
my name on your tongue, liked your rolling gait
across my heaving decks of libidinous undulations.

How long have you been gone? Ever think of me?
That spouse, that job, those abrading obligations
that walk you through years of your waning future
until – here you are: older, looking back, trying
to understand where it all went so fast, what's gone.

Somewhere within you, lover, I'm still moored.
You remember. My flag's still there to be unfurled.
Still in the amorphous hours asleep in your past,
tucked away inside me, is the soul of your world
loving life dearly, me dearly, life playing out fast.

Look: see us as we once were, that ocean singing,
that far away flowering of blossoms lost to time.
In memory's wishful imaginings, lay aside awhile
those drab inevitabilities that have been, still are:
my kiss is still on your heart, your love your star.

MEDITATION WHILE ON A BROAD REACH

Gossipy tongues of thread with a flicking flutter,
telltales don't lie. Believing their quick flitting
across jib or mainsail canvas, I trust their hinting
and loosen my mainsheet to straighten them out.
Easing a bit more wind, I sail half a knot slower,
riding relaxed, no desire to jibe or come about.

I eye the wind, whimsical, unreliable, quirky,
knowing light airs can push affairs one way
and then another, can freshen from cat's paws
to whole gale in a seeming second, inattention
shortening well-being (and maybe a life) at sea.
Ever on watch, I await oceanic fate patiently.

Am I resigned? Have I been taught? Do I
prosper from knowledge hard-earned along
history's lee shore? Smile at my resignations,
if you will, but I say to you there's a pleasure
in adjusting sails to prevailing wind, riding more
than driving, not racing when cruising avails.

There were seas I could've been borne across,
bays where exploration could've brought gold,
depths beneath me unplumbed, skies beckoning
with their sumptuosity of blue and high clouds,
but possibly made from a different mold than you,
I let safe breezes play gentle songs in my shrouds.

Risk-adverse? Not really: I've loved much,
and I've given freely of both heart and time
to salvage others while keeping my own boat right.

I've sailed such that prudent mariners applaud.
I've navigated celestially day and night toward
this broad reach relaxation, giving Zen the nod.

UNREQUITED

. . . it is
forbidden to love where we are not loved.
— Sharon Olds

I won't touch you, though everything
about this night was made for love: stars
large enough for a Broadway musical,
moon so wide and high Joe Howard
would've penned a Tin Pan Alley tune
taking advantage of its luster and bloom,
breezes so free fragrance of honeysuckle
would pierce walls of the remotest room
with perfume craftier than those of Paris.

 I won't kiss you, though everything
in this room screams, "Do it!" The floor
loves your feet, your weight, as do I, and
the walls bearing up the house would love
to bear you up, too, while couch and chairs
would worship your lithe, careless sprawl.
While they are busy with their own affairs,
houseplants gawk, even calm sansevierias
alarmed, wondering if lust will run amok.

I won't hug. I won't say sweet nothings.
Charmed to foolishness by your flesh,
I hang on, gripping with both my hands,
to societal standards coming to tatters
under your eyes, your lips and hips, and
I tell myself it's propriety that matters
even if my libido remains unconvinced.
I'll never taste you, nor will I hold you
with a love most would find misplaced.

One of us is too young or too old, and
there are laws, commitments, dogma
and dicta, not to mention cultural norms
that preclude my holding your hand,
and you don't know, and you don't care,
you thinking I'm just another guy who,
for no known reason you can fathom,
likes your company while you wait for
something to happen, something sublime.

DAYS OF 1968

They killed authentic heroes in 1968, and I watched it
on television. Again and again. Not Bobby and Martin,
but more chillingly before a shocked, draft-eligible educator
like me, Vietnam replayed its daily take of catastrophic politics
and war that once again would prove all the firepower
in the world can't kill an idea however silenced or mocked.

They took a naïve teacher out of a classroom of learning
to be untaught the humanities, to be armed, to be uniformed,
to be marched this way and that, back and forth, up and down,
to be ordered, trained, made buff, made of sterner stuff
than Empedocles, Socrates or Sophocles used in their creations,
to be a tool of battle and all its chaotic, robotic manifestations.

They took a naïve teacher out of a classroom of learning
to teach him more. They stripped him bare, physically and
mentally, threw his civilian make-up away, took love out of him,
and before they were done he was re-assembled as new clay,
pretty to look at in Navy working blues, slender in ass-tight pants,
young in mysteries of fatal attraction, tender fodder for war's muse.

Though I tried to forget love, some love remained. I strove
to be a sailor, yearned for acceptance among seafarers far more
seafaring than I, learned to guide passion beguiled by endless
sea and sky, earned commendations from every master and mate
for my cute performance as a military man dedicated to fight
for my country's obsessions without concern for personal fate.

My efforts weren't fake. I enjoyed my ship, riding the waves
with hunky companions, on watch at dawn's early light to see
in my ship's long wake strong spangles of fading stars abiding
into the morning then disappearing into white sea foam blown

alee, then to starboard, this way and that, as we raced war-ward
thrown with finality into harm's way like a slingshotted stone.

Aloha. My Bali Ha'i. Oahu. Pearl Harbor. Ford Island. And I
on watch when ashore for more men like me: loyal to a fault,
clean, buff, always unconsciously on the hunt for another guy
to couple with between duties and preparations for an assault
on the other side of the ocean, training then playing, training
again, playing again, always ready to set love or war in motion.

After a night of bliss comes a morning of responsibilities,
bare-ass fun ends at dawn, followed by armored service,
my warm flesh hidden safely, sagely under a cold uniform
and I salute at the quarterdeck coming aboard, salute as well
the flag, the Officer of Deck, the masculinity that is the norm
knowing Navy masculinity can produce both heaven and hell.

My days at sea are a preparation for violence, while my nights
ashore are a demonstration of what humanity is all about.
My days at sea are a camaraderie, working a well-oiled team,
leading, following, operating as an effective, efficient machine,
while my nights ashore find me kneeling in front of a boatswain
performing feats of eroticism my Navy recruiter had not foreseen.

Fight for my country? Sure. Die for my country? Of course.
If I live free, I'm willing to die for the land that makes it so,
though I know I speak remotely, far away from a bullet's stare.
Still, I swear courage with my crew, all sailors without remorse,
and I'll fight for my buddies who fight white-hot beside me, and
for those who are white-hot beside me in bed with equal force.

I was young then. Life was edible, delicious, bodies delectable
and ripe in their raw youth for copulation, ripe to be both
blowing and blown, too beautiful for any angry annihilation,
for a savage ripping apart and slaughtering of flesh and bone,

boys good only to make wishes on, boys lovely altogether,
boys too magical to be put to death, then forever to be gone.

To keep dominoes from falling, American boys were falling
by the thousands. Vietnamese boys were falling by the tens
of thousands, beautiful people much better suited for making
love than for taking up arms in war. Battles must be senseless,
for to touch, feel, smell, hear and see these fleshy wonders
would engender love immediately, leave the heart defenseless.

I was young then. Raw, not refined. Naïve, not experienced.
My mind open, not guarded. My thoughts simple, not subtle,
and I hadn't yet been trained to hate with a visceral will, I,
ready to give myself for play to an enemy who would plot
and wait, scheme, pretend, pounce, then kill and kill and kill,
I, a pacifist depending on others to save me from such an end.

More mascot aboard ship than a mate, more a puppy ashore
than an experienced seadog, I wanted pornography to be clean,
found much fodder for thought in pictures of guys as submissive
as me, enjoyed bondage fantasy as long as it wasn't obscene,
and while my country's culture would look on me with disgust,
I was an innocent, likeable guy, shy, decent and full of trust.

Safe in the bowels of ships, my attention on navigational plots,
on dials and meters and screens, I knew personal catastrophes
were wiping beauty off the face of the earth in the name of
this dogma or that, boys in their teens eviscerated, deboned,
beheaded, and I shied from thinking of their love going out
of the world and the world they leave behind cold, dreaded.

My letters home were upbeat lies. I couldn't write what
was being done as an act of war, and I couldn't write what
I was doing in shared beds ashore as an act of love. Humanity
does not fear guns. It fears love-making. Humanity is not

appalled by killing. It's appalled by two men forsaking norms
by sexually sharing themselves in ways healthy and thrilling.

On the surface of my uniform, I was exactly like everyone.
I was pretty, dedicated, superficial and could recite rules
I didn't believe were worth the powder to blow them to hell.
That powder, however, blew boys and men away, fools
fighting fools, economics and power blowing us all away,
although those of us left over ever respect those who fell.

I never fired a shot in anger. A thought that's chilling.
From my serene room with buttons, I needn't see mayhem
my finger, my hand, my grip, my cerebellum makes among
the lovely bodies of my pronounced enemies, the killing
taking place in an antiseptic elsewhere of my imagining,
the battlefield sanitized, massacre legal, spirit willing.

Is it just me? Is being gay an excuse to see my duty to fight
a lesser law than my duty to love? I had sex with more men
than I wounded or killed. I'm proud of that. I left more beds
with happy, satisfied men than I left sites with broken men
ready for stripping and rotting, bodies strewn about minus
heads. I slept with conflicted men who left me with a cry.

Forgive me when you read this. I never meant anyone harm.
I would've given aid and comfort to an enemy on cold nights,
slipping into bed for an exchange of love, no one asking why.
Passions of days of 1968 have calmed now, no one remembering
boys in oblivion, boys who once roved land, sea and sky, grand
in their flesh's honest promise that love seeds and war destroys.

Days of 1968 sleep soundly now in history's oceanic silence,
those guns, soldiers, sailors, and airmen all scattered, shattered
by the guns; soldiers, sailors and airmen of more recent wars
and the healthy bit of love-making shared among them all

are forgotten, too. So many magnificent young bodies fell fighting a losing war, but those dominoes, they did not fall.

LOVE CALL OF THE LAST GREAT AUK

*News Item: Although the last known sighting
of a Great Auk occurred on June 3, 1844,
when Icelandic fishermen bludgeoned to death
the last mating pair of the giant birds, individ-
uals probably continued to survive for a few
years more on lonely, isolated coasts of the
North Atlantic.*

Not a siren song of lilting larks, of tonal beauty,
more a clack and rasp, a choke half gasped,
echoing boldly across stark Greenland bays,
Icelandic fjords and arctic inlets, northern, cold,
and nonetheless a sound you cannot hear today.

No, there will be no rejoinder, no reply,
still crags echoless now to cacophonies of avian troth,
a summons to reproductive duty. There will be
no sounding from throats afire with longing
to slake desire in timeless unions human time has stayed.

He must have thought it strange, that spring day,
to stand deserted above a deserted beach,
to raise his head in unanswered call and say his love
to no other bird his voice could reach, to fall silent
listening for reply, to hear returning forever only
violent surf and illimitable wind under inviolate sky.

OLD SALT

I cannot rest from travel: I will drink
Life to the lees . . .
For always roaming with a hungry heart
Much have I seen and known . . . .

                                    – Tennyson

Not much I haven't seen here or there, in this or that,
not much kind or mean, thin or fat, round or flat
has escaped my eye as I rode what seemed like forever
in ships or strode what seemed like forever ashore.

Once a Slimy Pollywog, now a Trusty Shellback
many times a royal Son of Neptune ceremonially
crossing the line, I look back at all that's gone before
and revel in my service, my duty, glory and gore,

for the safety of a high-rise office, uniformity of
nine-to-five days, consistency of landsmen's ways,
brevity of adventure, would've killed me for sure,
and a sea-love takes me, makes me, and stays.

On an undulating ocean, everyone's alert, aware,
and over all slides the weather of a high, wide sky,
while beneath each keel rides legend, storied strife,
with ever-new challenges to be and do and dare,

and I have known them all, done them all, my life
a discovery, a mystery, an experience, a journey
from homeport to ports of call, from an awakening
to a confidence, from young spring to a fading fall.

I could tell a tale or two to sailors who even now
believe their experiences are the sum of the game.
I would tell them space and time at sea are infinite,
and from Adam to now love is eternally the same.

I've become old. Retirement stares me in the face.
I shall now walk away disappearing smiling, bold
in my going, content with my ocean odysseys, saying
little, passing on to a new offing with graying grace.

TRITON LIGHT

This light is dedicated to the safe return
of all those who go down to the sea in ships
— USNA Class of 1945*

In an awakening greening of an Annapolis spring,
perhaps early in morning or perhaps late afternoon,
or in an oncoming slumber of an Annapolis fall
when autumn intimates farewell and fallen leaves
bring to mind frost due soon, or in inclement weather
of an Annapolis winter storm when snowbound
midshipmen watch tossed spume icing seawalls,
or in an Annapolis summer's quiet vibrancy
when the human heart forgets buffeting squalls,
there, ever hailing homesick sailors returning,
ever welcoming mariners here no matter their loss,
signaling stalwart vigilance and dogged peace,
where the Severn River meets Spa Creek it calls
a message of permanent belonging to those who sail
the world's seas and who are filled with longing
for loves gone, youth fled, dreams chilled, times lost
that there is still Annapolis, still fresh, still a song
to be sung, a role to be played, a story to be written,
and Triton, son of Neptune, heralds home mariners,
summons experienced souls serving odyssey-long,
salt waters of twenty-two seas for salt water sailors
held beneath a green four-flashes-five-flashes light,
Triton, who would've made a good midshipman,
signaling love to comrades keeping honor bright.

MINOT'S LEDGE LIGHT, 1-4-3

Two miles off the Massachusetts coast, a granite column rises coldly,
sharply spear-like from a growling ocean to strike at slate-gray sky,
storm-tossed seas' incrustations of salt streaking from high up
on the glass canister holding a second-order Fresnel lens back down
to the lowly rounds whose ponderous tonnage bolts the dark base
to minacious Minot's Ledge on which the thunderous Atlantic sounds.

Like all lighthouses, this one is approached by sailors with bated breath,
for hidden under ominous swells lie sunken chunks of implacable stone
whose sly invisibility is betrayed by the running tide's rumbling moan
that translates to any listening ear as the parlous knells of sudden death.
Even on a calm night, no one sane would risk a ship disemboweled
by sailing near this cursed ledge once warned by its bold, blinking light.

Given the danger, it's an incongruent message of hope winking seaward:
one flash, a pause, four flashes, a pause, and then three – the same
syllable count as "I love you," one, then four, then three, and romantics
asea and ashore smile, move closer to one another, then hug and kiss,
finding wry humor coming from a tower above a granite catastrophe
that flashes above appalling, potent agonies such a calling out of bliss.

May it be so in our lighthouses of the heavens. May they flash love, too,
intergalactically in Morse code or semaphore, English or sign language,
or in an alien patois spoken by intelligences yet to sail through celestia
incognito on voyages of discovery to the Milky Way. May their stress
be relieved upon seeing "I love you" revealing the tenor of our wisdom.
May, in danger's heart, we humans think love. As we touch, let us bless.

RESPONSE TO W. S. MERWIN'S "UNKNOWN SOLDIER"

facing us under the helmet
a moment before he is killed
he is a child with a question
— W. S. Merwin

Face under the helmet has moist lips
and bedroom eyes, doe-like eyes,
so one may surmise hatred found him
before love did. Dicta and dogma's lies
have urged him on to the heroic deed,
his erotic need being war's first victim.

In answer to his question, war took away
his gun, stripped him bare, lubricated him
with sweat and blood, had him prostrate
by other young bodies prepared the same,
the truth becoming painfully obvious as
war's eclectic error-terror turned flame.

Bed or battlefield? Bed of battlefield.
Pillows or stones? Pillows of stones.
Sheets or shrouds? Sheets of shrouds.
War revealed flesh, bones. Bullets spoke
to him in reprimand: Don't entertain a
question whose answer you cannot stand.

WHEN YOUR SHIP COMES IN

I hope it's raining on that day,
a time of gloom, perhaps of loss,
of lost purpose, lost way, doom
alone seeming to be your future,
when what was right is wrong,
what's young is old, play is sad,
groaning is song, gold is gray,
and nothing can make you glad,

so when it docks, you're stunned
by health and wealth coming down
the gangway, a profusion of fame
waving hello and smiling, beauty
saying nothing will be the same,
love, love, calling you by name.

LAST LINES FROM THE STARBOARD WATCH:
"I STAND RELIEVED, SIR"

I watched in the winding long-life hours the whole night through
and kept a log truer than time.
Without a line taken back, tale unaltered from earliest beginnings,
I'll close this book ever in darkness, relieved of the watch at last.
And now, dawn moments from the farthest rim,
before blue, I go below for sleeping.
I pause numb from the length of incessant hours,
eight bells in my ears tonight by the steel bridge rail,
and I think on love in the darkness that never fails,
and love floats away from my grey ship slipping darkly on a glass sea plain.
Love lies sleeping on the smooth sea floor
caught silver perhaps in the light of some late star.
Love lies turning back in the heart of me as if the sea spoke of it and beckoned,
and love sinks slowly to the black bottom of the whole world
unnoticed by oceans and ships and men asleep on a night fully alone.
Love, as heavy as a stone, it is, finally let go.

DESPERATE JOURNEY

Warship red-right-returning,
where have we been, you and I, since we first set out together?
Did our starred and sun-crossed banner fly white and scarlet stripes
above virgin island harbors waking tropically in blue seas,
waking naked as our erotic youth would have them wake,
aroused and supple every one of them, in restless, resistless heat?
Were our hearts so much in love with new-found darkness running westward, too,
that, ever on watch in the dark-blue light of ocean evenings,
we sang old songs and told tales of lusts long past to a glistening sea?
And did we ride on stunning waves from Tonga south
on breathless worlds tumbling low and deep beneath our deep-plowing bow?

And were sudden gusts and whoosh of air really but a keening of a chastening wind
as we luffed along in our pride, on our way toward becoming loveless,
having sported wantonly from the shallows of our own red birth
into adulthood of glib lusts and depths of wetness and God denied?

Home port in pearl-light burning, open your arms
that through a time have been locked in prayers for the safety of our souls.
Your sons are now delivered, O Ye Harbor, back to a love that never bade them go.

Once, I thought of you, Mother of the Homeland,
when there on fields of endless sheen we star-fixed through celestial night
past Antipodes, where tender in the dark's soft kiss,
moist lips of our own brief youth, for one sweet moment, bid us home.

LINES FOR HORACE BRISTOL'S PHOTO OF A NAKED WWII PBY BLISTER GUNNER

After stripping off clothes, he dove
into slaying seas to save a fellow flier,
returning to his post and staying nude,
his PBY under fire from enemies lying
along Rabaul's coast, and by doing so,
he enflamed both fighting and desire.

Eros at war, a beautifully nude love
manning twin 30-calibre machine guns
made for death, not lust, and how sad
that is, for sea water glistens on skin
that steals a viewer's breath and who
would ever harm him must be mad.

He stands erotically heroic, as well as
heroically erotic, his intense steel gaze
through the clear Plexiglas blister
scanning the seas for enemies. One
sees war's immense lunacies framed
in that photograph: warm flesh bred

for copulation, bare-ass, ready for bed,
caught in hatred and battle, bodies
meant for ecstasy instead sought by
bullets to lay them dead like cattle,
doing what devils would do, as if we
needed our own Armageddon to rue.

Incongruity and irony are rife here
as they are in so much of humanity,
yet the ingenuity and naiveté of life

overcome the odds and humans make
love somehow, though all their kind
is threatened by their gods and strife.

Run your eyes softly, slowly over him.
He won't mind. Like Keats's youth
painted on a Grecian urn, he's frozen
in time regardless of what you will.
Love yearns. Did he live? However
your desire burns, he'll be forever still.

WAR POET

NOTES

A historical note on "Vice Admiral Harold G. Bowen, Jr., Reflects"

Vice Admiral Bowen served as President of the U.S. Navy's Court of Inquiry into Commander Lloyd Bucher's January 23, 1968, surrender of the naval electronic surveillance ship Pueblo to North Korean gunboats without firing a shot. Bucher's surrender, purportedly to save the lives of his 82 crew members, was anathema to Bowen who felt the honor and long-term safety of the country had been compromised by an act that had been more cowardly than humane. Bowen recommended a general court-martial for Bucher, as well as punishment for other officers in Bucher's chain of command. His recommendations, however, were politically unappealing to civilian leaders at the time and were countermanded by Secretary of the Navy John H. Chafee. Commander Bucher was never disciplined. He completed his Navy career and died on January 28, 2004. Vice Admiral Bowen, holder of the Distinguished Service Medal, the Legion of Merit and the Bronze Star, retired near Fort Myer and died on August 17, 2000. After the Court of Inquiry, the two men never met again.

ACKNOWLEDGMENTS

I gratefully acknowledge first publication of the indicated poems in these excellent publications:

War, Literature & the Arts – War Poet

White Pelican Review – Ode to War

Atlanta Review – Thoughts on a Suicide Bomber's Cowardice

Borderlands: Texas Poetry Review – Love's Triage

Poet Lore – Washing My Enemy's Feet

Off the Coast – Love Call of the Last Great Auk

Proud to Be: Writing by American Warriors, Volume 5, Southeast Missouri State University Press – Response to W. S. Merwin's "Unknown Soldier"

ABOUT THE POET

Rob Jacques served in the U.S. Navy during the Vietnam War, specializing in anti-submarine warfare and cryptography. He taught seapower, government, and English at the United States Naval Academy as an officer-instructor before becoming a civilian security specialist with the Department of the Navy. Emily Dickinson, Robert Frost, and James Merrill enhanced his interest in metaphysics and strengthened his resolve to work with rhyme and meter. He lives on a rural island in Washington State's Puget Sound with his husband, a fellow naval officer. They met and fell in love while stationed together on active duty.

ABOUT THE PRESS

Sibling Rivalry Press is an independent press based in Little Rock, Arkansas. It is a sponsored project of Fractured Atlas, a nonprofit arts service organization. Contributions to support the operations of Sibling Rivalry Press are tax-deductible to the extent permitted by law, and your donations will directly assist in the publication of work that disturbs and enraptures. To contribute to the publication of more books like this one, please visit our website and click *donate*.

Sibling Rivalry Press gratefully acknowledges the following donors, without whom this book would not be possible:

TJ Acena	JP Howard	Tina Parker
Kaveh Akbar	Shane Khosropour	Brody Parrish Craig
John-Michael Albert	Randy Kitchens	Patrick Pink
Kazim Ali	Jørgen Lien	Dennis Rhodes
Seth Eli Barlow	Stein Ove Lien	Paul Romero
Virginia Bell	Sandy Longhorn	Robert Siek
Ellie Black	Ed Madden	Scott Siler
Laure-Anne Bosselaar	Jessica Manack	Alana Smoot Samuelson
Dustin Brookshire	Sam & Mark Manivong	Loria Taylor
Alessandro Brusa	Thomas March	Hugh Tipping
Jessie Carty	Telly McGaha & Justin Brown	Alex J. Tunney
Philip F. Clark	Donnelle McGee	Ray Warman & Dan Kiser
Morell E. Mullins	David Meischen	Ben Westlie
Jonathan Forrest	Ron Mohring	Valerie Wetlaufer
Hal Gonzlaes	Laura Mullen	Nicholas Wong
Diane Greene	Eric Nguyen	Anonymous (18)
Brock Guthrie	David A. Nilsen	
Chris Herrmann	Joseph Osmundson